DINOSAURS
IN THE SKY

by Dougal Dixon

Gareth Stevens Publishing
A WORLD ALMANAC EDUCATION GROUP COMPANY

C O N T E N T S

The pioneers 4

Early flying reptiles 6

The discovery of
the pterosaurs 8

Solnhofen —
pterosaur paradise 10

The earliest pterosaur 12

Big heads 14

Soft coverings 16

The most famous 18

Heads & crests 20

The biggest 22

The first bird 24

Chinese "Gang of Three" 26

Toward modern birds 28

Abandoning flight 30

Since the dinosaurs 32

Did you know? 34

More books to read 34

Web sites 34

Glossary 35

Index 36

Please visit our web site at:
www.garethstevens.com
For a free color catalog describing Gareth
Stevens' list of high-quality books and
multimedia programs, call 1-800-542-2595
(USA) or 1-800-461-9120 (Canada). Gareth
Stevens Publishing's Fax: (414) 332-3567.

Library of Congress Cataloging-in-Publication Data
available upon request from publisher. Fax (414) 336-0157
for the attention of the Publishing Records Department.

ISBN 0-8368-2918-2

This edition first published in 2001 by
Gareth Stevens Publishing
A World Almanac Education Group Company
330 West Olive Street, Suite 100
Milwaukee, WI 53212 USA

This U.S. edition © 2001 by Gareth Stevens, Inc.
First published by ticktock Publishing Ltd., Century
Place, Lamberts Road, Tunbridge Wells, Kent TN2
3EH, U.K. Original edition © 2001 by ticktock
Publishing Ltd. Additional end matter © 2001 by
Gareth Stevens, Inc.

Illustrations: John Alston, Lisa Alderson,
Simon Mendez, Luis Rey
Gareth Stevens editor: David K. Wright
Cover design: Katherine A. Kroll
Consultant: Paul Mayer, Geology Collections
Manager, Milwaukee Public Museum

Printed in Hong Kong

1 2 3 4 5 6 7 8 9 05 04 03 02 01

IN THE SKY

WING AND A PRAYER

The earliest flying reptile known was the Late Permian *Coelurosauravus*. It looked very much like a lizard, but its ribs were extended to the side and supported gliding wings made of skin. The modern flying lizard of Malaysia glides in exactly the same manner as *Coelurosauravus*.

KING OF THE SKIES

By Late Triassic times, gliders like *Coelurosauravus* had been replaced in importance by the pterosaurs. These famous flying reptiles were the first vertebrates to adapt to a life of active flight. They appeared at about the same time as the first dinosaurs and became extinct at the end of the Cretaceous Period. Pterosaur wings were made of reinforced skin stretched out on an arm and an elongated fourth finger.

EARLY BIRDS

Birds such as this *Sinornis* appeared about halfway through the time of the dinosaurs, evolving from the dinosaurs themselves. Birds continue to thrive and are the main flying vertebrates today. Their wings are made of a bony structure consisting of some of the fingers fused together and supporting feathers that fan from the arms.

THE PIONEERS

While the dinosaurs, fish, and mammals were colonizing the land and the sea in prehistoric times, the sky above was buzzing with activity. Early flyers were simple organisms, but nature gradually came up with more complex designs. First came the insects, which continue to flourish today. Next came the flying reptiles, gliding creatures that evolved from ground-living, lizardlike animals. These reptiles were replaced in importance by the pterosaurs, probably the most famous of the ancient flying reptiles. Finally, the first birds appeared halfway through the time of the dinosaurs and have continued to rule the skies to this day.

AMBER PERFECTION

The best fossils come from amber preservation. When an unwary insect gets stuck in the sticky resin that oozes from tree trunks, the resin engulfs the insect and preserves it perfectly. When the tree dies and becomes buried over a long period of time, the resin solidifies and becomes the mineral we call amber. The 1994 film *Jurassic Park* was based on the premise that foreign DNA could be taken from biting insects preserved in amber to recreate the creature that was bitten. While this might not be possible today, it is an exciting concept.

THE FIRST KINGS

Meganeura was like a dragonfly but much larger — the size of a parrot. Its wings were typical insect wings, consisting of a thin sheet of chitin supported by a network of rigid veins. *Meganeura* lived in the Carboniferous Period, not long after insects first evolved.

CARBONIFEROUS/PERMIAN	TRIASSIC	EARLY/MID JURASSIC	LATE JURASSIC	EARLY/LATE CRETACEOUS
354-290/290-248 MYA	248-206 MYA	206-159 MYA	159-144 MYA	144-65 MYA

SOLAR POWERED

Kuehneosaurus, a gliding
reptile that existed in western
England in the Late Triassic, was very similar
in structure to *Icarosaurus*. There were about a
dozen wing supports (about half the number of
the earlier *Coelurosauravus*), suggesting that the
wings were longer and narrower and probably more
maneuverable. The skin of the wings was probably
rich in blood vessels, and the wings may have helped
warm up the animal in the sun like a solar panel.

LONG LEGS

Late Triassic *Sharovipteryx* from central
Asia was a small lizardlike animal about
the size of a sparrow. It had the most
ridiculous-looking hind legs, each one
longer than the complete length of the
body. These long legs only made sense
when scientists noticed the imprint of
a membrane of skin stretched between
the legs and the middle of the tail.

SHAROVIPTERYX IN FLIGHT

When alive, *Sharovipteryx* must have been able to glide using
the wings on its hind legs. This would not have been a very
stable type of flight, but it was probably efficient to transport
the reptile from one tree to another. Small skin flaps on the
forelimbs would have helped control the flight. With the wing
membrane stretched on elongated limbs, *Sharovipteryx* must
have resembled a back-to-front pterosaur. Some scientists have even
suggested that it may have been among the pterosaurs' early relatives.

EARLY FLYING REPTILES

The simplest kind of flight is a gliding flight — one that needs little muscular effort. All that is required is a lightness of body and some kind of structure that catches the air and allows the body to be carried along upon it, like a paper airplane. In modern times, we see this structure in flying squirrels, flying lizards, and even flying frogs. A number of flying reptiles populated the skies in Permian and Triassic times, and each one evolved independently from different reptile ancestors.

LONGISQUAMA

This fossil of the flying reptile *Longisquama* comes from Late Triassic central Asia. It had a completely different type of flying mechanism. A double row of long scales stuck up along the backbone, each scale forming a shallow V-shape along its midline. When spread, the scales would have overlapped like the feathers of birds (which appeared 60 million years later) to give a continuous gliding surface.

SCALES

A FAMOUS FIND

Three schoolboys in New Jersey discovered a famous specimen of Late Triassic *Icarosaurus*. The partial skeleton shows it to have been a lizardlike animal with long projections from its ribs. The angles at which the rib extensions lay suggested that the wings could have been folded back out of the way when the animal was at rest. Several decades after the discovery, one of the finders realized that under U.S. law the specimen belonged to those who made the discovery, and the specimen is now lost to science, having disappeared into a private collection.

PERMIAN	TRIASSIC	EARLY/MID JURASSIC	LATE JURASSIC	EARLY/LATE CRETACEOUS
290-248 MYA	248-206 MYA	206-159 MYA	159-144 MYA	144-65 MYA

SWIMMING PTEROSAURS

In 1784, some scientists put forward the idea that pterosaurs were not flying animals but swimming animals. This theory influenced many scientists and artists, including Johann Wagler, whose 1830 sketch (left) suggested that pterosaurs were an intermediate stage between mammals and birds.

DEVILISH PTEROSAURS

In 1840, British geologist Thomas Hawkins published a book on the fossil sea reptiles (the ichthyosaurs and plesiosaurs) that had been discovered up to that time. The frontispiece of the book was an engraving by John Martin, an English painter of biblical and historical subjects. It was a nightmare scene in which he depicted monstrous ichthyosaurs, plesiosaurs, and pterosaurs that resembled bat-winged demons.

FURRY PTEROSAURS

A surprisingly modern interpretation of pterosaurs was drawn in 1843 by Edward Newman. He regarded pterosaurs as flying marsupials. Although the mouse ears are inaccurate, the furry bodies and the predatory lifestyle are in keeping with how we now regard these creatures.

VICTORIAN TERRORS

The concrete pterosaurs (or "pterodactyles" as they were then called) erected on the grounds of the Crystal Palace in south London in 1854 tell us that most Victorians still viewed these creatures as winged dragons. These statues were more delicate than the surrounding statues of dinosaurs and sea animals, and unfortunately most were badly damaged or destroyed by the 1930s.

THE DISCOVERY OF THE PTEROSAURS

The first pterosaur fossil to have been scientifically studied was an almost perfect skeleton from the lithographic limestone quarries of Solnhofen, Germany, discovered between 1767 and 1784 (*see pages 10–11*). Although the skeleton was nearly complete, it was impossible to compare it with any animal alive at the time, so the find remained a mystery. Seventeen years later, the French pioneer naturalist Baron Georges Cuvier guessed that it was a flying reptile. Since that date, scientists have come up with many different ideas of what pterosaurs were and how they lived.

JURASSIC BATS?

English geologist Sir Henry De la Beche produced a drawing in 1830 showing animal life in the Jurassic (then called Liassic) sea of southern England. Life in the sea consisted of swimming reptiles, fish, and ammonites. In the air were flying pterosaurs, which De la Beche depicted as batlike creatures, with their wing membranes stretching all the way to their feet.

THE MODERN QUARRIES

Centuries ago, Romans excavated the fine limestone from the Solnhofen quarries to make tiles and paving stones. In the 18th century, the fine-grained surface of the rock was found to be ideal for printing. This discovery led to the rapid expansion of the quarries. Despite the fact that these quarries are famous for their fossils (not only of pterosaurs, but of early birds, small dinosaurs, lizards, and a whole host of marine animals), it takes the removal of a vast volume of rock to find one worthwhile skeleton.

NORTHERN EUROPE

SHALLOW WATERS
(MODERN SOUTHERN
GERMANY)

REEF

TETHYS OCEAN

SOLNHOFEN

Over millions of years, the surface of Earth has changed due to the action of plate tectonics, the name given to the activity that occurs beneath Earth's surface. Hot magma rises, forcing our planet to tear on the surface and separating previously joined landmasses. In Late Jurassic times, the area of southern Germany, including Solnhofen, lay in the shallows along the northern edge of the Tethys Ocean. This ocean separated Europe from Africa. Today all that is left of the Tethys is the Mediterranean Sea and the drying puddles of the Black Sea, the Caspian Sea, and the Aral Sea, all flanked by the mountains that were pushed out of the ground as the continents collided.

ANATOMY OF A LAGOON

Along the edge of the continental shelf to the north of the Tethys Ocean, a vast reef of sponges grew in deeper waters. Remains of this reef can now be found stretching from Spain to Romania. As it approached the surface, this reef stopped growing as the sponges died and coral reefs started to grow on top of them. Eventually, a series of lagoons was formed between the reef and the land. Low islands lay across the lagoon, and these were arid, with only a few scraggly plants. The stagnant water in the lagoon became poisonous and killed any animal that swam or fell into it. Because fine sediment was accumulating below, these animals were preserved almost perfectly at the bottom of the lagoon.

TRIASSIC 248-206 MYA	EARLY/MID JURASSIC 206-159 MYA	LATE JURASSIC 159-144 MYA	EARLY CRETACEOUS 144-97 MYA	LATE CRETACEOUS 97-65 MYA

SOLNHOFEN - PTEROSAUR PARADISE

Solnhofen in southern Germany has produced a treasure trove of finds — fossils in such wonderful condition that every detail of even the most delicate of organisms can still be seen. The rock is made of very fine particles and was formed under conditions totally lacking in oxygen, so no further decay took place. The technical name that geologists give to such fossil occurrences is *lagerstatten*. Only about a dozen such sites are known, and most people regard Solnhofen as the best in the world.

THE HEADLESS ONES

Many of the pterosaur fossils found at Solnhofen are without their heads.

The probable reason is that when the pterosaurs died they fell into the shallow waters along the northern edge of the Tethys Ocean.

When the pterosaurs landed on the lagoon, they floated at the surface for a while because their bodies were so lightweight.

While lying on the surface, their floating bodies began to decay and their heads, being the heaviest part, fell off first.

Eventually, after their heads had fallen off, the rest of the pterosaurs' bodies sank to the lagoon floor, where they were quickly covered by fine sediment.

LOW ISLANDS

LAGOON

POISONED ANIMALS

LIMESTONE

SPONGES

CORAL REEFS

NARROW WINGS
PRODUCING ACTIVE,
FLAPPING FLIGHT

THE FANTASY

Many works of fiction, including the film *One Million Years BC,* show pterosaurs carrying away heavy prey like human beings in their feet or their jaws. Even if human beings had been around at that time, the pterosaurs would have been unable to do this without severely disrupting their center of balance.

AN EDUCATED GUESS

Two good fossils of *Eudimorphodon* are known. They both have the wings folded to the body, but the wing membrane has not been preserved. Nor is there any direct evidence of a furry pelt. We can, however, guess what the membrane and the fur were like by comparing the fossils with pterosaurs that were better preserved (*see pages 14–15*).

LONG TAIL

TRIASSIC 248-206 MYA	EARLY/MID JURASSIC 206-159 MYA	LATE JURASSIC 159-144 MYA	EARLY CRETACEOUS 144-97 MYA	LATE CRETACEOUS 97-65 MYA

EUDIMORPHODON

Eudimorphodon had all the physical attributes of the rhamphorhynchoids. It had long, narrow wings made of skin supported by rods of gristle and a wing span of about 3 feet (1 meter). Because of its variety of teeth, it could easily catch and eat fish, and its furry body kept this creature warm and helped make possible its constantly active lifestyle.

SHORT
WRIST
BONES

TEETH OF
DIFFERENT
SIZES

FURRY
BODY

THE EARLIEST PTEROSAUR

The pterosaurs were the most important of the flying animals in Triassic, Jurassic, and Cretaceous times. Once they evolved, they quickly adopted all the features that were to remain with the group for the rest of their existence. Pterosaurs fall into two groups. The more primitive group — the rhamphorhynchoids — had long tails, short wrist bones, and narrow wings. Appearing in Triassic times, they were the first to evolve.

The other group — the pterodactyloids — evolved later, toward the end of the Jurassic.

WING MUSCLES

Pterosaurs must have had a flying action like that of modern bats or birds (right). The arrangement of their shoulder bones and wing bones show that the muscles facilitated active, flapping flight.

CATCHING PREY

Many pterosaurs caught fish, and, judging by its teeth, *Eudimorphodon* was one of them. The balance of the animal in flight was so delicate that it would not have been able to fly with a fish in its mouth. The pterosaur had to have swallowed the fish immediately to get it to its center of balance.

DIMORPHODON SKELETON

The skeletons of *Dimorphodon* fall to pieces and are crushed easily, because they are made up of the finest struts of bone. Nevertheless, two good *Dimorphodon* specimens have been found, both of them now in the Natural History Museum in London.

JURASSIC SKIES

Above the Early Jurassic shorelines the air was thick with wheeling pterosaurs. They were all of the long-tailed rhamphorhynchoid type. Within a few million years these creatures would be replaced by a new pterosaur group — the short-tailed, long-necked, long-wristed pterodactyloids.

BIG HEADS

Rhamphorhynchoid pterosaurs ruled the skies during the early Jurassic Period. The earliest Jurassic pterosaur known was discovered in 1828 by the famous professional collector Mary Anning. It was given the name *Dimorphodon* because of its two types of teeth. Scientists today are still in disagreement over many of its features. These disagreements are typical of our lack of knowledge of the pterosaurs in general.

BRILLIANT BEAK

Dimorphodon had two different types of teeth that were good for grabbing and holding slippery prey such as fish. The skull was very high and narrow and consisted of windows separated by fine struts of bone. The sides of the head were very likely brightly colored for signaling, just like the beaks of modern tall-beaked birds, such as puffins or toucans.

ON THE GROUND

We know that pterosaurs like *Dimorphodon* were very adept at flight, but we are not sure how they moved around when they were not flying. The old theory was that pterosaurs crawled like lizards, while some scientists saw them as running on their hind legs like birds, with their wings folded out of the way. However, footprints in lake sediments from South America attributed to pterosaurs show the marks of the hind feet walking in a narrow track, with marks seemingly made by the claws of the forelimbs in a wider track on each side. This suggests that pterosaurs were walking upright, using the arms like crutches or walking sticks. A final theory suggests that because of their similarity to bats, perhaps they did not come to the ground at all but hung upside down from trees.

TRIASSIC 248-206 MYA	EARLY/MID JURASSIC 206-159 MYA	LATE JURASSIC 159-144 MYA	EARLY CRETACEOUS 144-97 MYA	LATE CRETACEOUS 97-65 MYA

SOFT COVERINGS

WING STRUCTURE

The wing membrane of a pterosaur was stiffened by fine rods of gristle that fanned out from the arm and hand to the wing's trailing edge. The pattern of the gristle stiffening is the same as the arrangement of a bird's flight feathers and the supporting fingers of a bat's wing.

Most fossils are of sea-living animals, because sea-living animals have a better chance of falling to the seabed and eventually becoming entombed in sedimentary rock. However, many pterosaurs lived in coastal areas or around lakes and fell into the water when they died. Sometimes they were fossilized in environments that preserved the finest of details, such as wing membranes and fur.

A MODERN INTERPRETATION?

Many think that birds are the modern equivalent of the pterosaurs. The pterosaur has more in common with the modern bat than with any bird, however, particularly with its fur and membranous wings. Pterosaurs and birds shared the Cretaceous skies, but bats did not evolve until pterosaurs died out.

THE BEST PRESERVED

This *Rhamphorhynchus* from the Solnhofen deposits in Germany is one of the best preserved pterosaur fossils we have. Even the structure of its wing membrane is visible.

TRIASSIC 248-206 MYA	EARLY/MID JURASSIC 206-159 MYA	LATE JURASSIC 159-144 MYA	EARLY CRETACEOUS 144-97 MYA	LATE CRETACEOUS 97-65 MYA

HOW WERE THE WINGS ATTACHED?

A great deal of uncertainty surrounds the question of just how the pterosaur's wings were attached to the animal. Some scientists think that the wings stretched from the arms and fourth finger to the body and did not touch the hind limbs. Other scientists think that the wings were attached to the hind limbs at the knee. Others feel that the wings may have stretched right down to the ankles.

ATTACHED TO THE BODY   ATTACHED TO THE LEGS   ATTACHED TO THE ANKLES

FURRY PTEROSAUR

The fossilized remains of the rhamphorhynchoid *Sordes*, discovered among late Jurassic lake deposits in Kazakhstan in 1971, proved what many paleontologists had thought for a long time — that the pterosaurs were covered with hair. The sediment was so fine and the fossilization was so complete that not only was the wing membrane preserved, but fibrous patches were visible on the whole of the body, except for the tail. The diamond-shaped flap of skin at the end of the long, stiff tail was probably used for steering or for balancing as the animal flew.

When the British scientist Charles Darwin visited the Galapagos islands in the 19th century, he was struck by the variety of different beak shapes among one species of finch. Different shapes supported different lifestyles — heavy beaks for cracking seeds and short beaks for pecking insects, and so on. This revelation trigged Darwin's theory of evolution — the idea that, over millions of years, creatures could evolve to adapt to their surroundings. The variation in shape of the various *Pterodactylus* species fits in perfectly with Darwin's theory.

PTERODACTYLUS KOCHI

PTERODACTYLUS ELEGANS

PTERODACTYLUS ANTIQUANS

DIFFERENT HEADS, DIFFERENT FOODS

Several different species of *Pterodactylus* ruled the skies, each one adapted to a particular lifestyle and to eating a particular food. The smaller species with tiny teeth were probably insect eaters, while the bigger forms were most likely fish eaters. Six species are currently acknowledged, all discovered in Solnhofen. We used to think that there were far more, but many of these finds have subsequently turned out to be juveniles of known species.

TRIASSIC 248-206 MYA	EARLY/MID JURASSIC 206-159 MYA	LATE JURASSIC 159-144 MYA	EARLY CRETACEOUS 144-97 MYA	LATE CRETACEOUS 97-65 MYA

THE MOST FAMOUS

It is *Pterodactylus* that gives the pterodactyloid group its name. In fact, pterosaurs are commonly referred to as "pterodactyls." The pterodactyloids dominated in Late Jurassic times, but there have been several different types found dating from this time, so their evolution must have been under way somewhat earlier.

PTERODACTYLUS FOSSIL

As with *Rhamphorhynchus*, the best specimens of *Pterodactylus* have been found in the limestone deposits of Solnhofen. They clearly show the details of the skeleton and occasionally the imprints of the wing membranes. Sometimes there is even the imprint of a throat pouch similar to that of a pelican. Other remains of *Pterodactylus* have been found in similarly aged rocks on the south coast of England and in the dinosaur-rich deposits of Tanzania in Africa.

PTERODACTYLUS IN FLIGHT

Most agree that pterodactyloids originally evolved from rhamphorhynchoids, but *Pterodactylus* does display several differences from the group. Its head and neck are longer than in the rhamphorhynchoids. The head meets the neck at a right angle, rather than in a straight line, and its skull is more lightly built. It has a short tail, with no steering or flying function, and its long wrist bones mean that the three fingers of the "hand" are farther down the wing.

A QUESTION OF CRESTS

Many pterosaurs had spectacular crests that allowed them to signal to one another and identify members of their own species.

Pteranodon, with its backward-pointing crest, is the most famous of the crested pterosaurs. Its crest may have helped it steer as it flew.

PTERANODON

Tropeognathus had semicircular crests on its upper and lower jaws. This crest arrangement may have helped divide the water as the pterosaur dipped into the waves for fish.

TROPEOGNATHUS

TAPEJARA

Tapejara was characterized by a tall, bony crest at the front of its skull, probably supporting a flap of skin behind.

TUPUXUARA

Tupuxuara had a crest that consisted of a vast plate of bone reaching up and beyond the back of the skull. It was full of blood vessels and so must have been covered by skin. Perhaps it had a heat-regulating function as well as being used for display.

HEADS & CRESTS

irds are in great abundance today. They range from perching birds and swimming birds to wading birds and hunting birds. Modern birds have a variety of different heads and beaks — deep, strong beaks for cracking nuts; long, pointed beaks for probing mud; short, sharp beaks for pecking insects; and hooked beaks for tearing flesh. This variety was just as pronounced among the pterodactyloids. During their time on Earth, they diversified into different types, with different head shapes to suit different lifestyles.

HIDEOUS FIND

One of the most grotesque of the pterosaurs was *Dsungaripterus*. It had a beak like a pair of upturned forceps, a battery of crushing, toothlike, bony knobs at the back of the jaws and a crest that stretched from the back of the head to the snout. It was a large pterosaur with a wingspan of more than 10 feet (3 m). *Dsungaripterus* was the first pterosaur discovered in China.

DSUNGARIPTERUS RESTORED

We can usually tell how an animal lived and what it ate by looking at its jaws. *Dsungaripterus*, which we think lived in Late Jurassic and Early Cretaceous Africa, probably ate shellfish. The narrow, pointed jaws could have been used for digging out shellfish from rocky crannies, and the shells would have been crushed by the toothlike knobs in the back of their jaws. The crest could have been brightly colored and was probably used for signaling other pterosaurs.

TRIASSIC 248-206 MYA	EARLY/MID JURASSIC 206-159 MYA	LATE JURASSIC 159-144 MYA	EARLY CRETACEOUS 144-97 MYA	LATE CRETACEOUS 97-65 MYA

PTERANODON SKELETON

This partial skeleton of the giant pterosaur *Pteranodon* was found in Cretaceous rocks in Kansas. It shows a skull fragment, the bones of the wing finger, and the complete hind legs. The whole skeleton was extremely light in weight, and the bones had openings to allow oxygen into air sacks connected to the lungs. We see this system in modern birds.

QUETZALCOATLUS

PTERANODON

ARGENTAVIS

A FLIGHT OF MONSTERS

Pteranodon has long been thought of as the largest of the pterosaurs. The biggest species of *Pteranodon* had a wingspan of about 30 feet (9 m). In the 1970s, however, remains from an even larger pterosaur were found in Upper Cretaceous rocks in Texas. It was given the name *Quetzalcoatlus*, after the flying serpent from Aztec mythology. All sorts of estimates were made about the size of this beast. The current estimate is that it had a wingspan of about 36–39 feet (11–12 m). The biggest bird known is the condorlike *Argentavis* from Argentina, which existed around 35 million years ago. It had a wingspan of 25 feet (7.5 m). Among living birds, the royal albatross has the biggest wingspan, reaching 10 feet (3 m).

THE BIGGEST

Pteranodon was discovered in the 1870s in the Upper Cretaceous beds of Kansas. It had a wingspan of more than 30 feet (9 m). This discovery occurred before the age of powered aviation, and science was astounded by the idea that anything this large could fly. Today its size seems fairly modest when we compare it with more recent discoveries.

THE BIGGEST — FOR THE MOMENT

The current record holder is *Arambourgiania*, a pterodactyloid that may have had a wingspan of about 39 feet (12 m). It had an extremely long neck, and when the neck bones were first found they were thought to have been the long finger bones that supported the wing. The original name given to this creature was *Titanopteryx*, but scientists had already given that name to something else, so its title had to be changed.

THE SMALLEST — FOR THE MOMENT

At the other end of the scale, tiny *Anurognathus* holds the record for the smallest known pterosaur. It had a wingspan of about 2 feet (50 centimeters). Its short head contained little peg-like teeth that were ideal for catching and crushing insects. Despite its short pterodactyloid-like tail, it is actually a member of the more primitive rhamphorhynchoids. Only one skeleton has been found, in the Late Jurassic Solnhofen deposits (*see pages 10–11*).

TRIASSIC 248-206 MYA	EARLY/MID JURASSIC 206-159 MYA	LATE JURASSIC 159-144 MYA	EARLY CRETACEOUS 144-97 MYA	LATE CRETACEOUS 97-65 MYA

THE FIRST BIRD

In 1859, Charles Darwin published *The Origin of Species* and created a sensation. How could animals have evolved into different types over a long period if they had all been created at one time, as it says in the Bible? The scientific community found itself in opposition to the overpowering influence of traditional biblical teaching. Then, two years later, a remarkable fossil was discovered in the quarries of Solnhofen (*see pages 10–11*). It was obviously a dinosaur, but it featured bird's wings and was covered with feathers. Here were the remains of a creature that appeared to represent a stage in the evolution of birds from dinosaurs. Today, few scientists dispute the notion that *Archaeopteryx* (as this creature was named) evolved from dinosaur ancestors.

FEATHER

The first *Archaeopteryx* fossil to be found was no more than a feather. By itself, it looks like nothing unusual. It is a perfectly conventional flight feather as found on a modern bird. The main support is a vane that is off-center, showing that it is from a wing and used for flight. The filaments forming the vane of the feather had rows of hooks that enabled them to connect with one another and give stability — just as in a modern bird. A downy portion at the base provided insulation — also as in birds. About a year later, the first partial *Archaeopteryx* skeleton was found.

VINDICATING DARWIN

Eight *Archaeopteryx* fossils have been found so far, all from the Solnhofen quarries, ranging in quality from a single feather to an almost complete bony skeleton with feathers. One was found in a private collection, having been misidentified as the small dinosaur *Compsognathus*. This specimen did not show the feathers, and the misidentification points out the resemblance between primitive birds and their dinosaur ancestors.

THE LIVING ARCHAEOPTERYX

Had we seen *Archaeopteryx* in life, fluttering away from us, there would be no doubt in our minds that we were looking at a bird, though a rather clumsy one. However, a closer look would reveal a set of toothed jaws, as in a dinosaur, instead of the usual bird beak. The tail appeared to be paddle-shaped, unlike a modern bird's muscular stump with a bunch of feathers. This tail was a stiff, straight rod, like a dinosaur's tail, with feathers growing from each side. The final oddity would be the claws, three of them protruding from the leading edge of the wing. All in all, *Archaeopteryx* would have appeared part bird, part dinosaur.

COVERTS   PRIMARIES

CLAWS   SECONDARIES

THE WING

The wing of *Archaeopteryx* was no halfway measure. Apart from the clawed fingers, it was identical in structure to the wing of a modern flying bird, with the elongated fingerlike primary feathers, bunched secondaries, and coverts streamlining the whole structure. The wing muscles would have been weaker than those of a modern bird, since there was no strong breastbone to anchor them. But the flying action must have been the same.

TRIASSIC 248-206 MYA	EARLY/MID JURASSIC 206-159 MYA	LATE JURASSIC 159-144 MYA	EARLY CRETACEOUS 144-97 MYA	LATE CRETACEOUS 97-65 MYA

CAUDIPTERYX'S ENVIRONMENT

Caudipteryx (foreground), part of the Chinese "Gang of Three," lived in an environment like the one shown above. Forests of conifers and ginkgoes, with an undergrowth of ferns and cycads, provided refuge and food for many different animals in Late Jurassic and Early Cretaceous China. Lizards and small mammals scampered through the undergrowth, and little feathered theropod dinosaurs hunted between the trees. The air was colonized by birds (some resembling modern types), while on the ground raced several different half-dinosaur, half-bird creatures.

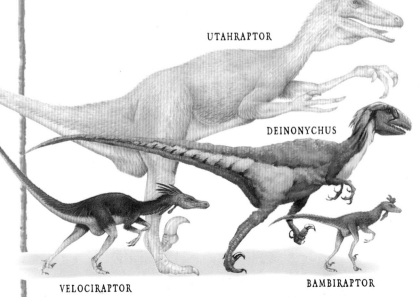

UTAHRAPTOR

DEINONYCHUS

VELOCIRAPTOR

BAMBIRAPTOR

MANIRAPTORAN DINOSAURS

The group of meat-eating dinosaurs known as the maniraptorans has always been viewed as birdlike. Attempts have been made to put them on the ancestral tree of the birds, but the problem is that, being Late Cretaceous dinosaurs, they lived much later than *Archaeopteryx*, which most scientists consider the first bird. Perhaps the maniraptorans evolved from *Archaeopteryx* or *Archaeopteryx*-like birds that lost their ability to fly. If that were true, they would have been very much like the Chinese "Gang of Three."

CHINESE "GANG OF THREE"

Across the contemporary European-Asian landmass, where China's Liaoning Province now lies, a series of forest-shrouded inland lakes produced fossils that were just as spectacular as those from Solnhofen. These include three kinds of animal that, like *Archaeopteryx*, show the evolutionary connection between birds and dinosaurs. Only recently, with improved scientific exchanges between China and the West, has their significance been fully appreciated.

SINOSAUROPTERYX

One of the little dinosaurs present in Liaoning Province was *Sinosauropteryx*. It seems to have been covered with fur or feathers. The fossil preservation is so good that a kind of downy fuzz is visible around the bones. Although there is still some dissent, most scientists are convinced that this represents a covering of "protofeathers," structures partway between hair, like that of a mammal, and feathers, like those of a bird.

SINOSAUROPTERYX FOSSIL

Only the downy covering on this skeleton shows *Sinosauropteryx* to have been related to the birds. Apart from that, it is pure meat-eating dinosaur. The long legs and tail show it to have been a swift-running animal, while the short arms displayed three claws. Three skeletons of *Sinosauropteryx* have been found, and their stomach contents show that they hunted lizards and small mammals.

HALF-BIRD, HALF-DINOSAUR

Another small animal was *Protarchaeoteryx*. It was about the same size as *Sinosauropteryx*, but it had a short tail and much longer arms. It was also covered with fuzz, and although the only skeleton found was very jumbled, there seemed to be long feathers along the arms and tail. The feathers on the arms would have given a winglike structure, but it would not have been sufficient to give the animal any power of flight.

TRIASSIC 248-206 MYA	EARLY/MID JURASSIC 206-159 MYA	LATE JURASSIC 159-144 MYA	EARLY CRETACEOUS 144-97 MYA	LATE CRETACEOUS 97-65 MYA

THE FIRST BEAK

Confuciusornis is the first beaked bird that we know of. A beak is a much more practical, lightweight alternative to the heavy teeth and jaws of a reptile. It consists of a sliver of bone, sheathed in a lightweight, horny substance that combines strength with lightness. Anything that reduces weight is an advantage to a flying animal.

ALULA

FLIGHT CONTROL

Eoalulavis, from Early Cretaceous lake deposits in Spain, is the first bird that we know to have carried an alula. An alula is a tuft of feathers on the leading edge of the wing, more or less where our thumb is. With very small movements of this structure, the passage of air over the wing can be altered considerably, and this makes flight much more controllable. Although all modern birds have this feature, fossils of *Eoalulavis* are unclear about whether the bird had other advanced features, such as a beak or a pygostyle.

CONFUCIUSORNIS FOSSIL

Many hundreds of fossils of *Confuciusornis* have been uncovered at the Liaoning site in China. Some are so well preserved that the details of the plumage are clear. Some have long tail feathers, like those of a bird of paradise, while others have none. This suggests that, like modern birds, the males had much more flamboyant plumage than the females.

TRIASSIC 248-206 MYA	EARLY/MID JURASSIC 206-159 MYA	LATE JURASSIC 159-144 MYA	EARLY CRETACEOUS 144-97 MYA	LATE CRETACEOUS 97-65 MYA

TOWARD MODERN BIRDS

For all its fine feathers, *Archaeopteryx* was still mostly dinosaur. It had a long reptilian tail, fingers on the wings, and a jaw full of teeth. Modern birds have stumpy tails called pygostyles supporting long feathers. Their wing fingers have completely disappeared, and they also have beaks instead of jaws and teeth. These are all weight-saving adaptations, evolved to make the bird as light as possible so that it can fly more efficiently. These features seem to have appeared at different times during the time of the dinosaurs.

A MODERN TAIL

Iberomesornis, a fossil bird from Upper Cretaceous rocks in Spain, is the earliest bird known to have a pygostyle tail. This structure consists of a muscular stump from which the tail feathers grow in a fan arrangement. The muscles of the pygostyle can spread the tail feathers out or bunch them together, helping control flight or make a display for courting purposes.

THE PERCHING FOOT

Birds that live in trees usually have feet in which the first toe is turned backward, enabling the foot to grasp a small branch so the bird can perch. An early example of a perching foot is found in *Changchengornis*, a close relative of *Confuciusornis* that is also found in the Liaoning rocks. This bird also had a hooked beak, suggesting that it was a meat eater, like a modern hawk.

Hesperornis was a swimming bird of Late Cretaceous North America. As big as a human, it must have looked something like a penguin, but with no forelimbs at all and a long beak full of teeth. This leg bone was found in chalk deposits in western Kansas.

THE DINOSAUR RE-EVOLVED?

A number of huge, flightless, hunting birds evolved around 65 million years ago, once the dinosaurs died out. *Phorusrhachos* of South America and *Diatryma* of North America were built along the lines of medium-sized meat-eating dinosaurs, with fast hind legs and fierce heads. *Titanis* (above) from Florida even had tiny clawed hands on the remains of its wings — almost as if a niche developed for dinosaur-shaped hunting creatures and evolution filled it with giant hunting birds.

KILLER DUCK

Bullockornis lived in Australia around 20 million years ago. It stood 10 feet (3 m) high and had a huge beak that was used for either cracking nuts or tearing flesh. An enlarged brain capacity suggests that the latter was more likely, since quick senses are necessary for hunting prey. *Bullockornis* was unrelated to the emus or the cassowaries or to any other type of flightless bird that exists in Australia today. Despite its dinosaur-like appearance, *Bullockornis* was actually a kind of duck.

ABANDONING FLIGHT

It seems to some scientists that often no sooner has a feature evolved than certain lines of evolution abandon it. As soon as flight evolved, some birds reverted to living on the ground. There are several explanations for this. Perhaps flightless birds evolved in areas where no dangerous predators lived on the ground, and so there was no need to fly, or perhaps food was more plentiful on the ground.

DEAD AS A DODO

Probably the best known of the extinct, flightless birds is *Raphus*, the dodo. The dodo evolved from pigeon stock into a ground-dwelling plant eater on the island of Mauritius. It survived there for thousands of years, as there were no ground-living predators. Everything changed, however, when humans arrived on the island, and the bird was wiped out within a few years.

PLANT EATERS

Not only were the shapes of the meat-eating dinosaurs reflected in some of the later birds, but bird versions of the long-necked plant eaters seem to have existed as well. *Dinorinis*, the moa, existed in New Zealand up to modern times. It thrived there because no ground-living predators lived in New Zealand — until human beings came along and wiped out the bird.

LATE CRETACEOUS 97-65 MYA	PALEOGENE 65-23 MYA	NEOGENE 23-1.8 MYA	QUATERNARY 1.8-0.01 MYA

SINCE THE DINOSAURS

The end of the Cretaceous Period was marked by a mass extinction. The birds were a bit luckier than other creatures. They lost three-quarters of their species, but the remaining one-quarter soon re-established themselves as the masters of the skies. As the mammals spread in the absence of dinosaurs, they also took to the skies. The bats developed successfully, and other mammal groups developed gliding forms. There were even gliding reptiles and amphibians. Throughout all this, insects continued to buzz, as they have done since Carboniferous times.

THE WEBBED WAY

The birds that survived the mass extinction went on to become the true masters of the skies. Birds today mostly fly, but they can also perch, wade, swim, and even burrow. *Presbyornis* was a long-legged wading duck that lived in huge flocks in North America around 65 million years ago. Although it had webbed feet, its legs would have been too long to allow it to swim. The webs probably developed to prevent it from sinking into the mud.

THE TRUE KINGS

Insects appeared nearly 400 million years ago and immediately evolved flying types. Few died out in the mass extinction at the end of the Cretaceous, and they are now far more diverse than any other group of creatures. Wings are the tough parts of an insect's anatomy, and it is mostly wings that have been fossilized. Occasionally the preservation is so good that the patterns and markings are preserved, although the colors have long since changed.

LATE CRETACEOUS 97–65 MYA	PALEOGENE 65–23 MYA	NEOGENE 23–1.8 MYA	QUATERNARY 1.8–0.01 MYA

MODERN GLIDERS

Today, gliding squirrels (right) float from tree to tree by means of flaps of skin (patagia) between their limbs. This is not a new development. In lake deposits in Germany, a well-preserved fossil of a gliding mammal around 23 million years old has been found. Only 4 inches (10 cm) long, *Eomys* shows evidence of patagia between the limbs. It was a kind of rodent, like a squirrel.

AN EARLY BAT

In the Early Tertiary , not long after the extinction of the pterosaurs, bats appeared. *Icaronycteris* would have been almost indistinguishable from modern bats. The only differences were the primitive teeth, the claw on the thumb and the first finger (modern bats only have a claw on the thumb), and the long tail that was not connected to the hind legs by the web of skin. In modern bats, the tail is completely joined to the wing membrane.

DID YOU KNOW?

• There are two kinds of flight in the animal kingdom — flapping flight and gliding flight. Flapping flight requires the animal to provide all the muscular energy to produce the flying action. Gliding flight simply requires the animal to have a certain shape of wing to soar through the air.

Flapping flight is seen in birds and in pterosaurs. This kind of flight may lapse into gliding flight, when, for example, a vulture soars on rising hot air, looking for food, or an albatross skims the wave surfaces of the ocean. Watch a pigeon in flight when it is courting. It flaps its way to a particular height, then glides downward as if on a roller coaster, and then flaps upward again. Presumably, the pterosaurs of old had similar habits, using a variety of flying techniques.

There are two types of gliding flight. In one type, the gliding action is initiated by the animal's own muscular efforts. Flying fish, for example, launch themselves into the air by swimming rapidly to the surface and using the movement of their strong tails to throw themselves out of the water. In the second type of gliding flight, the animal simply drops down from a high vantage point and, like a hang glider on a slope of air, uses its aerodynamic shape to take it where it wants to go. Flying squirrels, flying frogs, and the flying dragon lizards of Malaysia do this type of gliding to take them from a higher place to a lower place.

• Scientists disagree as to how bird flight evolved. Some say that primitive birds, such as *Archaeopteryx*, started as gliders. Others see these birds as essentially terrestrial creatures, launching themselves into the air by running quickly along the ground.

MORE BOOKS TO READ

Digging for Bird-Dinosaurs: An Expedition to Madagascar. Nic Bishop (Houghton Mifflin)

Feathered Dinosaurs. Christopher Sloan (National Geographic Society)

A Moment in Time with Sinosauropteryx. Philip J. Currie, Eva Koppelhus, and Jan Sovak (Troodon Productions)

Ornithomimus: Pursuing the Bird-Mimic Dinosaur. Monique Keiran (Raincoast Books)

Pteranodon. Discovering Dinosaurs (series). Daniel Cohen (Bridgestone Books)

Pterodactyls. Elaine Landau (Children's Press)

WEB SITES

Archaeopteryx: Taking Flight. *www.amnh.org/enews/verteb/v34.html*

The Pterosaur Home Page. *www.pterosaurs.net*

GLOSSARY

alula: a tuft of feathers on a bird's wing that helps the bird maintain control while in flight by influencing how air moves over the wing.

ammonites: extinct, mollusklike marine animals of the Mesozoic age that had flat spiral shells.

beak: the horny, projecting bill of a bird.

chitin: the organic substance that forms the hard outer shell of insects, arachnids, and crustaceans.

crest: a projection, such as a tuft of feathers or fur, on the head of a bird or some other kind of animal.

DNA: an acid inside every living cell that carries genetic information about individual heredity.

evolution: the theory that organisms change form and develop over long periods of time, so that descendants look or behave differently than their early ancestors.

filaments: fine, thin threads of material.

fossils: remnants or impressions of organisms from a past geologic age embedded in natural materials, such as rock or resin.

glide: to fly, or soar, on air currents without natural or mechanical propulsion.

hinterland: an area or region that is inland from a coast or at a distance from cities.

lagoon: a shallow body of water, especially one separated from the sea by sandbars or coral reefs

lithographic: capable of printing, copying, or otherwise producing an image, pattern, or impression.

magma: the molten rock material beneath Earth's crust that, when cooled, forms igneous rock.

mammals: warm-blooded, vertebrate animals, including human beings, that have hair or fur on their skin and nourish their young with milk produced in the mammary glands of the female's body.

membrane: a thin, pliable layer of tissue that covers or separates certain parts of an animal's body, such as its organs.

niche: a situation or activity well-suited to an organism's interests or abilities.

plate tectonics: the theory that Earth's continents once were a single landmass that drifted or was forced apart over billions of years.

plumage: the feathers of a bird.

pouch: a saclike structure beneath the beak of some birds for carrying food or on the abdomen of some marsupials for carrying their young.

pygostyle: the muscular, stumplike tailbone of some birds, which contains vertebrae that are fused, or joined, and which controls the movement of tail feathers.

quarries: large, open pits or excavations of land that are dug out to obtain stone, sand, or gravel.

reef: a ridge of rocks, sand, or coral at or near the surface of a body of water, usually only a short distance offshore.

reptiles: cold-blooded, egg-laying vertebrates, such as snakes, crocodiles, or turtles, that have scales or horny plates on their bodies.

sponges: primitive marine animals with porous skeletons that grow like plants and attach to surfaces underwater.

struts: bars or rods used to brace a structure against pressure along its length.

vertebrae: the segments of bone or cartilage that form an animal's spinal column.

INDEX

Africa 10, 19
amphibians 7,
 32, 34
Anning, Mary 15
Anurognathus 23
Arambourgiania
 23
Archaeopteryx 24,
 25, 26, 27, 29, 34
Argentavis 22
Asia 6, 7, 27
Australia 30

Bambiraptor 26
bats 8, 9, 13, 15,
 16, 32, 33
beaks 15, 18, 21,
 25, 28, 29, 30, 31
birds 4, 5, 6, 7, 8,
 10, 13, 15, 16,
 18, 19, 21, 22,
 24–32, 34
Bullockornis 30

Carboniferous
 Period 5, 32
Caudipteryx 26
Changchengornis 29
China 21, 26–27,
 28, 29
Coelurosauravus
 4, 6
Compsognathus 24
Confuciusornis
 28, 29
crests 20–21
Cretaceous Period
 4, 13, 16, 21, 22,
 23, 26, 28, 29,
 30, 32
Cuvier, Georges 9

Darwin, Charles
 18, 24
De la Beche,
 Sir Henry 9
Deinonychus 26
Diatryma 30
Dimorphodon
 14, 15
Dinornis 31
Dsungaripterus 21

Eoalulavis 28
Eomys 33
Eudimorphodon
 12, 13
Europe 10, 27
 England 6, 8, 9,
 14, 19
 Germany 10, 33
 Solnhofen 9,
 10–11, 16, 18,
 19, 24, 27
 Romania 10
 Spain 10, 28, 29
evolution 7, 13,
 18, 19, 24, 27,
 29, 30, 31,
 32, 34

fish 5, 9, 13, 15,
 18, 20, 21, 34
fossils 5, 7, 8, 9,
 10, 11, 12, 16,
 17, 19, 24, 27,
 28, 29, 32, 33

Hawkins, Thomas
 8
Hesperornis 30

Iberomesornis 29
Icaronycteris 33

Icarosaurus 6, 7
ichthyosaurs 8
insects 5, 18, 21,
 23, 32

Jurassic Period 9,
 10, 13, 14, 15,
 17, 19, 23, 26

Kuelmeosaurus 6

Longisquama 7

Malaysia 4, 34
mammals 5, 7, 8,
 26, 27, 32, 33, 34
maniraptorans 26
marsupials 8
Martin, John 8
Mauritius 31
Meganeura 5

New Zealand 31
Newman, Edward
 8
North America
 30, 32

Permian Period 7
Phorusrhachos 30
plesiosaurs 8
Presbyornis 32
Protarchaeoteryx
 27
Pteranodon 20,
 22, 23
pterodactyloids 13,
 14, 19, 21, 23
pterodactyls 8, 19
Pterodactylus 18, 19
pterosaurs 4–6,
 8–17, 19–23,
 33, 34

Quetzalcoatlus 22

Raphus 31
reptiles 4–9, 21,
 28, 29, 32
lizards 4, 5, 6,
 7, 10, 15, 26,
 27, 34
rhamphorhynchoids
 13, 14, 15, 17,
 19, 23
Rhamphorhynchus
 16, 19

Sharovipteryx 6
Sinornis 4
Sinosauropteryx 27
Sordes 17
South America
 15, 30
Argentina 22

Tapejara 20
Tertiary Period 33
Tethys Ocean
 10, 11
theropods 26
Titanis 30
Titanopteryx 23
Triassic Period 4,
 6, 7, 13
Tropeognathus 20
Tupuxuara 20

United States 7,
 22, 23, 30
Utahraptor 26

Velociraptor 26

Wagler, Johann 8

ACKNOWLEDGEMENTS

The original publisher would like to thank Advocate and Elizabeth Wiggans for their assistance.

Picture Credits: t=top, b=bottom, c=center, l=left, r=right
Lisa Alderson: 6b, 15b, 16-17c, 22l, 26b, 27t, 31bl. John Alston: 10l, 10-11b, 11tr, 12-13c, 13cr, 13b, 17t.
BBC Natural History Unit: 16cl. Corbis: 10t, 16b, 18c. Dr Peter Griffiths: 24t, 24b, 25r. Simon Mendez: 4-5b,
6-7c, 14-15, 15t, 18-19c, 20t, 27t, 28t, 29t, 29b, 30-31, 32l. National Museum of Wales: 9, 20b.
Natural History Museum: 5t, 8t, 12b, 14t, 18t, 23r, 31t. Paleontologisk Museum, Oslo: 6cl, 7cr, 28cr.
Luis Rey: 7b, 12tl, 19, 20-21c, 22-23, 24-25, 26t, 27bl, 30l, 32-33.

Every effort has been made to trace the copyright holders, and
we apologize in advance for any unintentional errors or omissions.